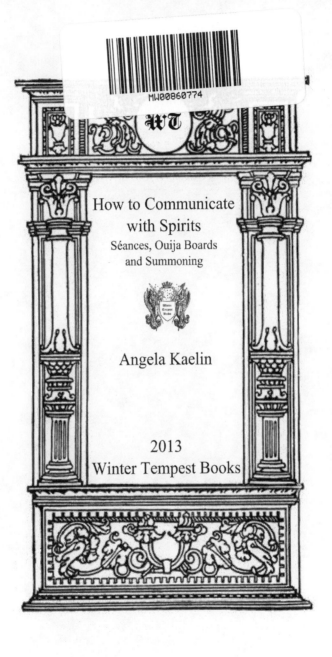

# How to Communicate with Spirits

Séances, Ouija Boards
and Summoning

## Angela Kaelin

2013

Winter Tempest Books

# DEDICATION

In honor of my grandparents.

# CONTENTS

ANGELA KAELIN

# CHAPTER 1
# THEORIES ABOUT SPIRIT COMMUNICATION

Despite the fact that spirit communication is an ancient practice and one that has been the subject of a lot of research in the past 180 years, no one really knows exactly how it works. But, in order to begin a study of spirit communication, it is important to have a model or a theory on which to base our exploration. A commonly accepted theory, which seems to have a basis in practice, is that there are different planes or bandwidths of existence and that communication can take place when the parties involved are mentally tuned to the same frequency.

According to the famous psychic and founder of the Theosophical Society, Madame Helena Petrovna Blavatsky in *The Secret Doctrine,* the life force energy on the physical plane was once much less dense. As the energy of this plane grew denser, it became more difficult for people in physical bodies to do some of the things they could do before, including communicating with beings on the other planes. As a result, most human beings have become trapped in their energetically dense physical bodies and are unaware of what exists outside their range of perception. Those individuals who can sense anything outside that dense physical range of energy are called "psychics."

We live in a sea of frequencies, whether we are aware of them or not. When an idea is written, spoken or thought, it has an energetic frequency which can be perceived by anyone who has the ability to intercept and interpret it. Whether between corporeal or incorporeal beings, spirit communication can take place in this way.

Language, itself, is an important means of spirit communication. Certain languages like Old Norse and Hebrew are more than just words, but symbols endowed with magical properties and were intended to be a means by which man could communicate with both the gods and one another.

According to surviving literature, spirit communication sometimes involved journeys to the dwelling place of the gods or spirits. For example, in the Norse sagas, the humans and gods went inside the earth to discourse in Hell. In the Greek tales, when inquiries must be made of the dead, the querent journeys across the River Styx. But more often, spirits are invoked or evoked through meditation, prayer or ritual.

Sometimes communicating with spirits is easily accomplished; yet at other times, it is very difficult and requires great patience. External factors such as astrological timing may be involved in the ease or difficulty of making a connection. The physical, mental and emotional condition of the people involved can, also, make communication more or less successful.

In all old civilizations, psychics as shamans and

healers performed a special function, much like that of a priest, among their people. It was their job to act as psychic mediums between the people and the spirits or gods. They often still exist among people whose cultures were not perverted by more modern, religious beliefs. This is the case among some Africans who commune with their ancestral gods. The most familiar of which to us in the West are the Orishas, the ancestral gods of the Voodoo tradition, which has its origins among the Yoruba-speaking people of West Africa. These spirits are fierce protectors, gentle teachers and powerful healers who once walked among the people and whom African psychics contact for information and assistance. Communication with them can occur through dreams, divination, prayer, channeling or ceremony.

Virtually any intelligent person has the ability to communicate with spirits, although it is often regarded as a special ability. This power is not the unique property of religious or spiritual leaders as some people have been led to believe.

In modern times, there has been a widespread, sustained attempt by tyrannical governments and religion to destroy these practices and even the practitioners. Psychics have been ridiculed, scapegoated, persecuted and murdered in large numbers throughout the world.

In parts of Western Europe and Britain at different times between about the 15th and the 18th centuries, there was a violent persecution of people who were suspected of not being loyal to the church or state, which were usually one tyrannical governing body. This period of time is known to many modern witches as "The Burning Times," because many innocent people who had property the state wanted to confiscate, who represented a threat to the establishment in some way or who just had the misfortune of having spiteful neighbors were tortured and many of them burned to death by religious and government officials. In the early colonies of New England, similar persecutions of people suspected of communicating with spirits and possessing supernatural powers occurred.

It was a difficult time for anyone whose beliefs differed from those of the government, the common religion or the dominant culture they lived in. Fortunately, attitudes toward tyrannical governments and dictatorial religions slowly began to change. By the late 18th and 19th centuries, it was acceptable to question the status quo in the West and a spiritual rebirth began, which was led by the Spiritualists whose goal was to learn the truth about life after death through research and experimentation. As a result, there is now a greater acceptability of psychics and psychic experiences of all kinds.

# CHAPTER 2
# THE INFLUENCE OF POPULAR MEDIA ON THE ACCEPTABILITY OF SPIRIT COMMUNICATION

In the West, the fascination with the subject of ghosts and spirits is centuries old and has never gone out of style. Although, popular perceptions about the subject have changed over the years, especially with the advent of mass print and other types of media.

Popular media both reflect and direct people's thoughts, beliefs and attitudes. As early as the 18th century, literature began to have a powerful influence on people's opinions about spirit communication.

The Gothic and subsequent Romantic literary period in England drew upon the work of Shakespeare while assimilating the very best influences of German literature with its tales of ghosts and pacts with the devil. These influences spread to American authors, most notably Washington Irving and Nathaniel Hawthorne.

This movement reached the height of its glory during the Victorian period as the belief in spirits and spirit communication was becoming increasingly socially acceptable, particularly among the upper social classes.

The Gothic period is said to have begun in 1764 with the publication of *The Castle of Otranto* by Horace Walpole, in which the affairs of a family of monarchs appears to be violently influenced by some unseen force. It was brought to its pinnacle with the publication of Ann Radcliffe's novel, *The Mysteries of Udolpho*, in 1794. In Radcliffe's work, the belief in spirits was widespread among the servant class, but characters of a higher social rank were far too sensible to give into silly superstition and ridiculed those who did.

This theme is seen again in the most famous works of Charlotte and Emily Bronte: Jane Eyre and *Wuthering Heights*. It is the servants of the house who hold occult knowledge about spirits while their betters remain skeptical of such superstition.

In fact, it is a running theme in the literature and history of England that the middle class, that solid body who worked the fields, became teachers, fought in wars, maintained vicarages and who become the overseers in factories during the Industrial Revolution, were the least likely to have any interest in the occult. Such preoccupations belonged almost exclusively to the lower classes and the titled upper echelon.

Tales of pacts with the devil can be traced back to the early Christian period. But, the English literary legacy of dealings with the devil began with the publication of Christopher Marlowe's *The Tragical History of Dr. Faustus* in 1604. It was based on the *Historia von d. Johann Fausten*, which was written by an anonymous German author and published in Frankfurt am Main in 1587. Marlowe's tale ends with Faust being dragged to Hell by demons, suggesting that any deal a man makes with the devil is doomed from the start because the devil will always prevail.

Subsequent works which made use of Faustian themes include works by American authors, such as Washington Irving who wrote *The Legend of Sleepy Hollow*, Stephen Vincent Benet who wrote *The Devil and Daniel Webster*, and Henry James who wrote, *A Turn of the Screw*.

From these works, the reading public might conclude that communicating with spirits, such as the devil, may result in peril to one's body, soul and property. For example, *The Devil and Daniel Webster* imparts the concept of the devil as a being concerned with contracts, litigiousness and the court system, however, in some American tales, the devil could be defeated at his own game.

The vampire, another kind of spirit who is a revenant from the grave with a lust for blood, was first impressed upon the mind of the public in 1819 with the publication of *The Vampyre* by John Polidori. This work became the foundation of the literary canon for vampire literature. It has, also, become the basis for belief or disbelief in vampires in English-speaking countries.

In the early 19th century, particularly in New York, it became acceptable and even fashionable to question Christianity. This loosening of the bonds of social and religious oppression paved the way for the Spiritualist movement, whose members largely came from affluent families. It began in 1848 with an investigation into the mysterious rappings heard by the Fox sisters, which led to a series of experiments that would influence religion, science, literature and popular thought for more than a century.

The Spiritualists experimented with many methods of spirit communication. From table rapping, they graduated to table tipping, the use of automatic writing planchettes and the development of the spirit board, popularly known as the Ouija. As a psychical research tool, it was used to connect with the spirits of loved ones, both living and dead, during the World Wars and to inquire into the nature of the world beyond this one. The Ouija hit the height of its popularity in the 1960s.

In recent years, television and film have had a profound effect on the public's opinion of spirit communication, especially with regard to the Ouija board. Sadly, its popularity and its reputation suffered after the release of an iconic horror movie.

The 1973 film, *The Exorcist*, forever changed how people perceived the Ouija board and afterward it became widely regarded as a portal to demonic possession. In the minds of people who get their information about the occult from popular movies, it is now commonly regarded as dangerous and the surest path to enslavement by the devil himself.

Subsequent horror movies, like W*itchboard,* released in 1986, served to solidify the dangers of Ouija boards in the mind of the public and thus began a new canon of belief. For example, people indoctrinated by this film believe the surest path to demonic possession is to use a Ouija board alone.

Although Ouija boards have not fared well in popular culture during the past 35 years, they are occasionally employed in conjunction with sophisticated equipment on paranormal investigation reality shows.

By contrast, witchcraft made great strides in popularity in the same period of time. Popular movies, like *I Married a Witch* and *Bell, Book and Candle*, were the forerunners that brought witches and their powers to the television screen on a regular basis between 1964 and 1972 with the airing of supernatural-themed television programs. Charming Samantha of *Bewitched* and Sabrina of *Sabrina the Teenage Witch* with her feline familiar Salem entertained television viewers between 1972 and 1974.

Witchcraft enjoyed a powerful resurgence in popularity with the release of the hit movie, *The Craft*, in 1996. This film aroused interest in the occult among many high school and college students and it even influenced the Wiccan religion it portrayed. Afterward, popular interest in all aspects of witchcraft and the occult grew rapidly. In 1998, the television show, *Charmed*, a series about three sister witches, ran its pilot featuring a beautiful spirit board. This show was so popular it ran for eight seasons.

Unfortunately, despite the mainstream popularity of the occult, in some parts of the U.S., both psychics and witches are still marginalized, even discriminated against in employment, generally treated unfairly and even forbidden to practice their skills because of anti-fraud laws.

ANGELA KAELIN

# CHAPTER 3
# PSYCHICS VERSUS THE STATE

In early 19th century New York, the Spiritualists opened the door to a renaissance of belief in spirit communication. By 1951 in England, they broke down the wall of Medieval Christian superstition once and for all with the repeal of the anti-witchcraft laws.

The Witchcraft Act was actually a succession of acts which defined the conjuration of spirits, spell-casting, divination and other practices common to witchcraft as a felony. These laws actually made the practice of holding a séance at one's private kitchen table a criminal offense. While the repeal of the Witchcraft Act was not a complete end to the persecution of psychics, it did lead to very great changes in both the U.K. and the U.S.

In both nations, psychics sought refuge in the mantle of religion. By the 1890s in the U.S., the Spiritualists had begun forming their own formal organizations and churches and they were gaining ground in England in terms of public opinion.

The Witchcraft Act was finally repealed because of the influence of English Spiritualists who exposed the sheer absurdity of such laws. Shortly afterward, witches slowly began coming out of the closet and a spiritual revolution was quietly underway.

The repeal of the Witchcraft Act paved the way for Gerald Gardner's publication of the book, *Witchcraft Today*, in 1954 and his founding of a religion to be known as Wicca. A different, more independent version of Gardner's Wicca took shape among people in the U.S. Much like Spiritualism, Wicca largely became a religion for women and when the social revolution of 1960s began, Wicca took its place among feminists, especially in the U.S.

In the U.S., Wiccans were able to win the right to officially call Wicca a religion through several court rulings. Although, the government itself really has no authority to define what a religion is or is not, it is a liberty they take to decide who receives certain legal privileges. Nonetheless, because Wicca is a form of witchcraft and because their practices involve the belief in communication with spirits and divination, it has helped make the U.S. a safer, more legally tolerant place for psychics.

By 1954 in England, Spiritualism was officially recognized as a religion, affording English psychics and mediums greater legal protection. Pagans, including Wiccans, still face discrimination in the U.K, but have, also, received recognition as a religion, which provides some legal protection for psychics, as well.

## Why is Spirit Communication Seen as a Threat?

Originally, the reason for the passage of the Witchcraft Acts in England was to eradicate the belief in such practices as spirit communication from the minds of the common people. In recent decades, the ostensible reason for similar laws is the prevention of fraud. But, this is obviously not the truth.

Laws preventing the practices of psychics are enacted not to protect the masses, but to protect the interests of the state. Heads of state have always tried to hoard this knowledge for themselves.

British monarchs have secretly sought after psychics, alchemists, wizards and astrologers while suppressing such practices among their people. For example, Queen Elizabeth I hypocritically sought counsel from her court astrologer and summoner of dubious angels, John Dee, yet during her reign the Elizabethan Witchcraft Act of 1562 was passed prohibiting "Conjuracions Inchauntmentes and Witchecraftes."

It is a generally accepted fact that Hitler's rise to power was facilitated by occultists. Yet, he made a point of eliminating psychics and astrologers during his reign, while he and leading members of his party are said to have consulted a psychic and stage magician named Erik Jan Hanussen, whom they later apparently murdered, possibly for knowing too much about their plans.

King Edward the 7th and Prime Minister Winston Churchill were said to be in consultation with famous occultists and members of The Golden Dawn, Dion Fortune and Aleister Crowley. Furthermore, various writers and researchers have reported finding information linking Crowley to the CIA, NASA and the Nazis, as well.

The connection between the British government's desire during World War II to use spirit communication for its own purposes while suppressing its use among the general population seems to be highlighted in England's prosecution of Helen Duncan, one of the last women to be convicted under the Witchcraft Act.

In 1941, during one of her séances in Portsmouth, a recently deceased sailor from the HMS Barham fully materialized. He told her that his ship had sunk as a result of enemy action. This fact was denied by the British government, however, it turned out that the ship had been sunk and the British War Office had not yet received this information. Duncan and her sitters were arrested, although not for fraud, but for conspiracy. She was accused of being a spy, was convicted under the Witchcraft Act of 1735 and spent nine months in prison.

In the United States, while laws are passed to prosecute psychics and movies are made to frighten the public or to make the idea of spirit communication seem ridiculous, government defense agencies have spent huge amounts of the people's money on psychical research.

For example, declassified documents from black defense projects in the U.S. reveal that the Stargate Project engaged in psychical research between 1970 and 1995. The Stanford Research Institute and The American Society for Psychical Research were involved in these projects. A specific protocol for clairvoyance was established, called "Remote Viewing," which is featured in the 2009 comedy film, *The Men Who Stare at Goats*.

It is a fact that the ability to communicate with spirits gives people power and access to important knowledge. Therefore, it may be that all of the propaganda against communicating with spirits has been part of a plan by governments and religions to hoard and concentrate their power and keep information out of the hands of the general public.

# CHAPTER 4
# TYPES OF SPIRITS

Information about the different types of spirits that may be encountered comes, not only from folklore, grimoires and sacred literature, but from research by psychics, magicians, Spiritualists and Spiritists. In recent years, hundreds of independent paranormal research groups have sprung up and many have documented and published the results of their investigations.

The following is a breakdown of different types of entities, however, it is necessarily over-simplified because the lines between many of these classifications are blurred. Gods are sometimes confused with demons, some angels are not all they seem and many spirits are changelings or shape-shifters.

**Gods and Deities:** Of course, the most common type of spirit people communicate with through prayers and visions and through the medium of priests and saints is an anthropomorphic "god" who may be called Jehovah,

Yeshua or Jesus, Allah and many other names. A lot of spirit communication that goes on occurs between man and some monotheistic god.

Prayers and mantras to Buddah and the gods of the Hindu pantheon are another example of widespread spirit communication.

Similar forms of communication go on between people and entire pantheons of gods, goddesses and demi-gods among pagans and neo-pagans. Africans, the Indians of North and South America and the aboriginals of Australia communicate with their deities through ritual, drumming, chanting, dreams and visions.

**Ghosts:** The most common type of spirit manifestation is the common household ghost. The experience of living in a haunted house is what propels many people's initial interest in spirit communication. There are natural questions about the nature of the haunting and who the spirit is that people want to answer.

Often with these hauntings, the first members of the household to notice the uninvited resident are children. Theories abound as to why children seem to be more apt to see ghosts than adults.

One reason for this may be that children have a large supply of personal life force energy, which the spirits require to manifest strongly. Another reason may have more to do with their lack of social conditioning. Young children are known for their blunt honesty and have not yet been conditioned to edit out that which isn't supposed to exist. So, when they see a ghost, their sub-conscious minds don't go into conditioned denial.

Most ghosts are the spirits of deceased human beings but some are deceased pets, especially cats. Many of them seem to interact with human beings in real time. These are the spirits with whom we may be able to establish communication. Many families live happily with ghosts just as the staff and clientele at many hotels, bars and other businesses do. In fact, some commercial businesses profit from having these spirits on hand who seem to enjoy interacting with their staff and customers.

But, some ghostly apparitions appear to take no notice of the living. Frequently, these hauntings are timed and are confined to a certain area. It's almost as if a sequence of events is playing out over and over again and the haunting is like the sound and audio impressions on a video recording. It is as if some emotion or thought has been impressed permanently into the ether in those locations.

Some ghostly hauntings are accompanied by music or the sound of doors opening and closing as if there is another person in the house moving from one room to another. These sounds may be faint or they may be startlingly loud.

Other hauntings involve physical phenomena such as items in a room being mysteriously moved from one place to another and items disappearing and reappearing. In extreme cases, household items may seem to leap off shelves and books and other objects fly across the room. Such noisy ghosts are called poltergeists and are more rare than other types of apparitions.

Ghosts can be associated with ordinary objects. For example, mirrors are frequently said to be haunted or to be portals to other dimensions. They are, also, attached to places including houses, prisons, mental institutions, dormitories, hospitals, cemeteries and churches.

And, sometimes they are associated with people. Although, spiritual attachments who overstay their welcome are sometimes creatures of a more insidious nature.

**Angels:** Angels have two basic forms: Dark and light. While both groups are angels, the dark angels or the fallen ones are usually called demons. Whereas, the light beings are generally willing helpers to mankind when called upon. When psychics see angelic beings they may appear kindly or fierce, but they radiate light.

The classification of 72 angels of light originated with the ancient Hebrews. Their names are given and their function is described in *The Kabbalah Unveiled* by S. L. MacGregor Mathers. There are other classification systems that divide the angels into orders. The main protectors of mankind and enemies of the fallen ones are the four archangels: Michael (also, called Mi-ki-gal), Gabriel, Raphael and Uriel.

Angels are a race of beings apart from humans, their name means "messenger." They are ancient beings endowed with great knowledge and courage. They are fierce protectors of human beings when they are called upon. They vanquish dark entities and have reportedly saved the lives of people in dire circumstances. Like their dark counterparts, certain angels perform particular functions including teaching astronomy, inspiring love, bestowing good fortune, healing, imparting beauty, inspiring the arts and assisting with divination.

There are, also, personal angels, which some people believe are assigned to guard individuals, especially children.

According to Aleister Crowley, everyone has a Holy Guardian Angel who is the person's "higher self" and serves as a source of knowledge and inspiration if you can only silence your mind well enough allow communication to take place.

**Demons:** Demonic spirits take on an incredibly wide variety of forms. Some are low-level parasites like "alcohol entities" that infest alcoholics and seem to peek out through their eyes or lurk around their heads and shoulders. People addicted to hard drugs frequently have similar attachments.

Included in this category are the shadowy apparitions

that radiate malevolence which appear both by day and night. They take different forms, but certain themes are reported more often like "the old hag," and "the hat man." The old hag is a frightening female and "the hat man" is an evil-radiating, masculine shadow that often appears to children. Others are impish little shadowy forms that can be seen out of the corner of the eye or heard scampering about the house at night. George Noory of the paranormal radio show, *Coast to Coast AM*, is credited with coining the term, "Shadow People," to describe these entities.

The word demon can be traced to the Greek world for demi-god or half-god. In ancient Hebrew and much older Sumerian lore, there are tales of non-human beings (angels, aliens or ancient inhabitants of this planet by different accounts) who mated with human beings. Demons may be the spiritual offspring of these unions or they may be the non-human entities themselves. Psychics see a wide variety of these creatures, their appearance varying greatly, some taking on partial animal forms while others appear more human. They can change their appearance at will, sometimes accidentally when their emotions overtake them or upon command when they are properly constrained.

At least, some of these demons belong to a hierarchy as described in *The Lesser Key of Solomon*, also, called *The Lemegeton* and *The Clavicula Salomonis* and as discussed in *The Goetia*. These and other demonic entities are usually summoned in rituals under the protection of the archangels who are their enemies. Demons and their light angelic counterparts are and army arranged in a hierarchy each dominated by 72 kings.

The dark angels may be the Nephilim, who are mentioned twice in the Hebrew *Bible*, in *Genesis 6:4* and *Numbers 13:33*. They are sometimes associated with the

Annunaki, the gods of the Sumerians. They are also called the Grigori and the Watchers.

Some of the high ranking demons are summoned by magicians to obtain knowledge about herbs, healing, alchemy, divination and all manner of secrets. Some demons are master architects who build structures for the summoner while others perform tasks like bringing him treasure from within the earth. Some seem to be willing performers while others must be threatened in order to obtain results. People who communicate with demons are, also, called exorcists because their purpose in summoning is to make the entities subservient and obedient to the summoner's will and never the other way around.

Remarkably, there are some magicians who do summon demonic entities in rituals for the purpose of allowing the demons to enter into their bodies or the bodies of children. Such rituals are described by Leo Zagami, a thirty-third degree free mason, high-ranking Illuminati Grand Master and the author of the book, *Le Confessioni di un Illuminato,* with regard to the practices of a faction of the Jesuits. A similar ceremony to summon particular spirits into the womb is described in Aleister Crowley's book, *Moonchild,* which is very revealing despite its fictional format.

There are many other demonic entities such as those listed in the *Necronomicon* by Simon, a book with some very obvious historical inaccuracies but which is, nonetheless, useful in drawing forth dark entities, sometimes inadvertently by the reader.

Queen Elizabeth I's court astrologer, John Dee and his scryer Edward Kelley communicated with spirits they called "angels" and documented a language called "Enochian," which they claimed was so powerful in manifesting spirits that it had to be stated in reverse, otherwise the entities would appear. Many people have called into question the nature of these angels, which seem to be of a darker nature.

**Fairies, Sprites, Sylphs and Salamanders:** They are intelligences associated with the four elements: Earth, water, air and fire. Elemental nature spirits are known throughout the world although, most notably the Celtic, Latin and Slavic nations, Spain and Japan. They figure heavily into the literature, lore and mythology of the ancient Germans, such as in *The Nibelungenlied.*

Fairies or "the fae" are any number of little people, which are especially plentiful in Celtic folklore. They are said to resemble humans, but are diminutive in size. They are sometimes depicted with pointed ears or colorful wings and are credited with being helpful to human beings, but, also, doing mischief.

Fairies, nymphs and gnomes are associated with trees, flowers and forests. The word, gnomes, comes from the Greek "geomus" meaning earth-dweller. People who are tuned into this range of frequencies sometimes see these entities around plants.

According to the alchemist Paracelsus von Hohenheim, undines and sprites are water fairies. They're associated with lakes, streams, wells and other bodies of water.

Mermaids and sirens are, also, water spirits usually associated with larger bodies of water. The most famous water sprite is Melusine, a shape-shifting mermaid who is said to have married a French Count of Anjou and produced three monstrous children with him, thus polluting the bloodline of the Angevins and the Plantagenets, who would later come to the English throne, much to the horror of 12th century England. They were called "the Devil's brood." This story was taken very seriously then and it was certainly not the last time that members of the royal family have been described as "not human."

Melusine is a name used to refer to other legends of beautiful maidens who married human men, mated with them and then were later revealed to have scaly fish tails instead of legs. If you look carefully at the logo of Seattle, Washington-based Starbuck's Coffee, you will see Melusine depicted with her two tails.

Sylphs are spirits of the air who live in the mountainous regions, the clouds and the upper atmosphere.

Salamanders are associated with fire and take the form of lizards. They are the most dangerous of all of these elementals. Paracelsus wrote: "Salamanders have been seen in the shape of fiery balls, or tongues of fire, running over the fields, or peering in houses."

Other spirits are genies, djinn, goblins, trolls, dragons and animal spirits. These spirits can be kind or cruel and they can bring good or bad luck, protection or knowledge.

The best way to get in touch with beneficial elemental spirits is by creating gardens with pretty fish ponds, little brooks, flowers and trees. Just as certain flowers and trees attract certain species of birds and insects, they also attract different kinds of elemental spirits. Bluebells, heather, pansies, peonies, roses and poppies are all flowers associated with fairies in folklore.

Decorate with figures representing the kinds of spirits you want to attract and make a point of regularly tending your garden while inviting good, kindly elemental spirits into it. Pause for a few moments and wait to see if you see, hear or feel them around you.

**Extra-terrestrials:** Some people have theorized that some spirits, in particular, demons and fairies are actually extra-terrestrials who may be from somewhere else or who may have always existed on or within this planet.

According to many eyewitness reports, E.T.s and U.F.O.s share the same abilities as spirits to suddenly appear or disappear, to change their form and to communicate psychically.

Our first inclination might be to dismiss some more fanciful types of spirits as fantasy or delusion, however, it is important to remember that the history of this planet is largely unknown. Archaeologists frequently find anomalies among skeletons of very large creatures resembling dragons and very small creatures similar to legendary trolls. It is possible that this planet, its interior, its waters and its atmosphere might be haunted by the spirits of any being that may have an interest here.

The common thread that runs through the accounts of all the different types of spirits is their inter-dimensional nature.

ANGELA KAELIN

# CHAPTER 5
# HOW TO SUCCEED AT ALL METHODS OF SPIRIT COMMUNICATION

To succeed at most methods of spirit communication, it is important for psychics to maintain good mental and physical health. In particular, physical mediumship requires the accumulation of a large supply of personal life force energy and bioplasmic energy.

This can be accomplished through both nutrition and specific techniques involving meditation and directed mental imagery. Techniques of maintaining a large supply of life energy are discussed in detail in the book, *Magical Healing: How to Use Your Mind to Heal Yourself and Others*. In general, learning multiple occult disciplines is beneficial to whatever spiritual practice you undertake.

When you are preparing for a session or find your energy supply lagging, use the following methods to keep your physical and bioplasmic energy bodies charged.

## How to Keep the Physical Body Energetically Charged

The subtle energy that spirits use to manifest in any way is supplied by the life force energy of the participants. A great supply of this energy is generated by a person who is in good health.

As much as possible, establish a healthy diet of live, raw foods including plenty of fresh fruits and vegetables. Try to avoid foods that drain your life force because they require a lot of energy from your body to process. Such foods are any that are cooked, pasteurized, processed or otherwise dead and devoid of necessary enzymes and life-giving energy.

Also, take the common sense precaution of not being under the influence of drugs or alcohol, especially, right before or during a session.

An electrolyte imbalance can, also, interfere with your ability to communicate with spirits and is sometimes the underlying cause of a failed session. If your electrolytes become imbalanced because of over-exertion, heat exhaustion or the flu, you will likely feel fatigued, disoriented and light-headed. In more extreme cases, you may, also, experience headaches and dizziness. When you have an electrolyte imbalance, simply drinking water does not seem to quench your thirst.

Use this simple electrolyte restoration drink recipe to quickly restore your body's balance:

## Electrolyte Restoration Drink

1 quart water
1/2 tsp. baking soda
1/2 tsp. sea salt
3 to 4 tablespoons raw sugar
1/4 salt substitute (potassium chloride)
3 to 4 tablespoons fresh lemon juice (optional)

Combine the above ingredients together and stir until dissolved. Serve as is or iced.

Take common sense steps to take care of your health. Reduce your stress level as much as possible and get sufficient sleep and exercise.

Do not engage in sessions or rituals for spirit communication when you feel tired or ill.

## How to Keep the Bioplasmic Body Energetically Charged

The physical body and the metaphysical body (or bodies) are inseparable. Disturbances in physical or mental health have a relationship to disturbances in the bioplasmic body; one affects the other for good or ill.

A gifted or well-trained psychic healer can see disturbances in these fields and balance them. If you are plagued by such disturbances, a genuine psychic healer or even a good Reiki practitioner can help.

Physical illness, shock and trauma can all lead to a depletion of this field and a weakening of the life force. Therefore, for your overall health as well as successful spirit communication, you will need to strengthen you bioplasmic (or auric) field.

**Here are some suggestions:**

Cleanse your aura before a session by bathing in a tub with one-half to one cup of sea salt and several drops of lavender oil.

Take a few minutes to relax and strengthen your auric field with this simple meditation: Visualize a white light, tinged with the stabilizing color of blue, pouring down through the top of your head and filling your entire body so that it flows out of your palms and finger tips in a never-ending supply.

The solar plexus, situated in the triangular shaped area beneath the rib cage, is where we experience fear. It is the center through which receive lower psychic signals, which are called intuition or "gut feelings." Disturbances in the solar plexus cause worry, obsessive thoughts and digestive disturbances.

To clear the solar plexus, relax and meditate while holding one of the following crystals over this part of your body: Citrine, amber, tiger's eye or yellow calcite. Breathe deeply and rhythmically as you visualize a white light, tinged with blue flowing through the crystal and into your solar plexus.

To balance the solar plexus and deeply relax, drink lemongrass tea. If you are suffering from anxiety, add a teaspoon of dried valerian root to your tea. Drink this two nights in a row before sleeping to induce muscular relaxation and help to clear emotional disturbances.

Drink a cup of ginger tea before bed time to reduce anxiety and enjoy a relaxing sleep. Ginger is a natural source of melatonin, a chemical produced in the pineal gland.

To strengthen the bioplasmic body through the power of the spoken word, say these words aloud: "The Holy Ghost is in me and all around me!"

Alternatively, say: "The Power of Odin [the Odic

Force] flows through me and all around me!"

Both of the above statements are very empowering. You can also obtain a rush of energy with the following simple visualization exercise:

Close your eyes, relax, sit or stand with your palms turned upward and imagine your entire body engulfed in an ultra-violet flame. This flame is purifying you and your bioplasmic energy field. It transmutes negative energy to positive and enables you to connect with the One, the Cosmic Consciousness, the All, God or whatever name you prefer. Hold this vision for three to five minutes or longer if you are able.

Meditating on the violet flame is so effective and so easy to do that it requires little more than your willingness to experiment with it, however, further description is given by Djwal Kul Kuthumi (the spirit of an Ascended Master) in the book, *The Human Aura: How to Activate and Energize Your Aura and Chakras.*

The importance of a maintaining healthy bioplasmic energy field cannot be overstated, especially now, because we live in a sea of electromagnetic frequencies produced by microwave towers, radio, satellite, television and other wireless communication systems.

We are, also, bombarded with increasing amounts of radiation and chemical poisoning in the food. It is very important for the psychic to keep the chakra system and the endocrine system in good order. The chakra system feeds etheric life energy directly into the physical body through the endocrine system.

The key gland of the endocrine system is the thymus, which is vulnerable to radiation. This gland controls metabolism and the body's energy level.

The pineal gland, which is associated with the third eye or ajna chakra, is necessary to more sophisticated spirit communication. It is vulnerable to poisoning from sodium fluoride and other additives intentionally placed in food and water.

The solar plexus is vital to lower forms of spirit communication involved in intuition and emotion. Psychic empaths operate mainly from this chakra center.

All of these energy centers must be balanced, which means each chakra must be functioning optimally, to supply energy to your endocrine system for it to work properly.

All psychics should strive for optimum physical health and try to avoid stress and emotional shocks. This may mean avoiding situations involving a lot of people or noisy activity. Many psychics and, in particular, empaths sometimes feel bombarded by the signals they pick up from other people and find it difficult to be in crowded places for a long time.

It appears that there is an attempt by powerful agencies to scramble the signals that psychics receive and to make spirit communication more difficult. An example of this is Ashtar Command, which is a communication signal being transmitted to discredit and confuse psychics who are able to connect with its broadcast. The broadcast is real and many of the people who are able to pick up this communication are genuine. But, it is a suspected PsyOp (Psychological Operation) perpetrated by black government agencies to disseminate disinformation to psychics within the New Age and U.F.O. research communities. This is possible because the signals that psychics receive and interpret during the course of spirit communication are very much like radio or satellite broadcast signals.

It is beneficial for psychics to refrain from watching television. The flicker rate and low frequency alpha waves television transmissions emit change the human brain wave pattern and put viewers in a hypnotically suggestible state, which they have no control over. Furthermore, watching television takes energy from you and leaves you feeling drained, lethargic and mentally foggy.

The excessive bombardment of waves and signals in recent decades may be an attempt to make spirit communication more difficult. If it is not a deliberate act, it is quite a coincidence, especially when taken in consideration with the effects of radiation and chemical poisoning on the human body. For this reason, it is very important for modern psychics to pay special attention to their diets, avoid chemical poisons, keep their mental focus and try to maintain a relaxed, emotionally balanced state.

## The Key to Success in All Spirit Communications

In all conscious attempts at spirit contact, it is necessary to cultivate and maintain a calm, focused state of mind. You must formulate and focus your intention. Eliminate anything that can interfere with your uninterrupted concentration. Then, state your intention silently or aloud.

The directing of your will is like navigating a sea of energies with your mind. It is like steering a ship's rudder in that it drives you wherever you want it to go, however, you must remember that yours is not the only mind in this sea of energies.

Other people, including spirits, have a mind and a will, also. You can only direct your own will; you cannot control the desires or the will of others. So, even formulating your intention and directing your will perfectly does not guarantee that you will end up at the destination you have in mind because there are other factors involved. But, frequent practice and making every attempt to perfect your technique will improve your abilities.

This following is a very important key to success in

all kinds of spirit communication whether it is through a traditional séance, a dumb supper, automatic writing or Ouija boarding: Give the spirit permission to use your personal supply of bioplasmic energy. Tell the spirit silently or aloud, "You may use my energy to manifest."

If you are working as a medium with inexperienced sitters, all of whom should be in good physical and psychological condition, they should be instructed to do this, as well. After all, their purpose at a sitting is not to be entertained, but to give their energy to the proceedings.

This is the case in ceremonial magic rituals, as well. Good spirits will not use your energy without permission and bad spirits may try, but, usually they cannot.

Most types of spirit communication are not dangerous for healthy people with the exception of deep trance mediumship in which ectoplasm is produced. Although, spirit communication should not be undertaken by those who suffer from mental illness because it may aggravate an existing condition.

# CHAPTER 6
# HOW TO CONDUCT A TRADITIONAL SÉANCE

The Spiritualist Churches teach people how to become mediums. Members practice telepathy, psychometry and mediumship and the readings and séances they perform at their meetings are intended to bring messages of hope and comfort. If you have the opportunity to attend one of their séances, you should do so because sitting with a circle of accomplished mediums is the quickest way to learn.

Although, two or three friends who are committed to the goal of mediumship development can achieve the same success through persistence and dedication.

Séances succeed more often when they are conducted at the same time, at the same place with the same small group of committed people. Sittings should not include spectators. Furthermore, skeptics of the type who try to trick, play pranks or debunk mediums should never be allowed to attend.

Séances can be conducted during the day or night, however, generally the evening hours are preferred because people's minds are more at rest and there is likely to be less environmental noise, especially as the night progresses.

Some mediumship development groups have each member take turns acting as the medium. Other groups are headed by experienced mediums who have an established reputation and who always play this role at sittings. Ideally, a group should only consist of people who have a good personal chemistry with one another and who support the purpose of the mediumship development group.

The medium directs the proceedings and determines how the room is to be arranged, who is to be seated where and other details. The purpose of the sitters is to support the medium and to help generate sufficient life force and bioplasmic energy for communication to occur.

Bright lights may interfere with the participants' ability to go into a deeply relaxed state, therefore, the lights are usually dimmed and sometimes a single lamp or a candle is used to provide some illumination. How bright or dim the room is during a session should be decided upon by the medium with input from the sitters. It is important for both the medium and the sitters to be comfortable. Attention should, also, be paid to the temperature of the room so that it is neither too cold or too hot.

In popular portrayals of séances, people are often depicted sitting around a table, sometimes holding hands or touching outspread fingers upon the table. This was done to keep the participants "honest" in cases where the authenticity of the séance might be called into question. When people gather for a serious session, they do not need to hold hands or touch each other.

In some groups, it is forbidden for anyone but the medium to speak during a session. This should be decided upon by the medium.

The medium should not be touched or startled while in trance and, especially, in the course of producing a physical manifestation. It has been reported that mediums have died after being startled during the production of ectoplasm, however, this is an extremely rare occurrence.

Practiced mediums can go into a trance quickly and begin connecting with spirits. Sometimes results are produced fairly quickly, however, it is common to sit in a meditative state for a very long time before success is achieved.

In your first endeavors, you may want to attempt to make content with your own higher self or with a helpful spirit who can act as your "control" or helper.

If you are not connecting after half an hour or so, take a break. Drink plenty of fresh water and have a light snack of raw fruits or vegetables. Then, after 10 or 15 minutes, resume the session again.

You may begin each session with an invocation such as those used with Ouija board sessions or by simply stating your purpose so that everyone knows the session has begun. Some mediumship development groups use guided imagery to help the entire group go into a highly relaxed, meditative state before the actual proceeding begins.

## Guided Imagery to Help the Group Enter a Highly Relaxed State

The following is an example of the kind of guided imagery that is used to begin a session. Recite the following hypnotic induction in a low, evenly modulated voice:

*Settle into your chair and adjust your body until you feel comfortable.*

*Now, slowly, slowly allow your shoulders to drop...*

*Notice how your arms feel heavy...*

*They hang loosely from your shoulders.*

*Gently close your eyes and, as you do, you feel very light, like a helium balloon.*

*If any worries or cares come to your mind, acknowledge them briefly, then allow them to float away... so far away that you cannot sense them anymore... they simply disappear from your awareness.*

*You are completely relaxed and nothing matters at this moment...*

*...and, you begin to feel more and more relaxed... more relaxed than you can ever remember.*

*Slowly take a deep breath...*

*And, slowly let it go... and as you let it go... you now find that you are even more relaxed than before...*

*Slowly, take another breath...*

*....and slowly, slowly let it go... and as you do, you sink even more deeply in to deep relaxation...*

*With every breath you take, you become more and more relaxed... deeper and deeper... every time you breathe... you become more relaxed than you've ever been before.*

*You are now so very comfortable and relaxed that you feel your whole body sinking into the chair.*

*Every muscle in your body from the largest to the*

*smallest is now more relaxed than you can ever remember. You drift down, down, like a leaf falling gently from the branch of a tree, down, down into deeper and deeper relaxation. Your arms and your legs and your hands and your feet... every muscle is relaxed.*

*You are aware of a sense of deeply calming peace... you feel peace deep inside you... you feel perfectly calm and perfectly content.*

*The muscles of your back relax now... and as you continue to breathe in and out, you are aware that with every breath that you release, you sink deeper and deeper into a relaxed sleep.*

*And, with every breath you sink deeper and deeper into this warm, relaxed sleep. Your legs now feel very heavy... as heavy as lead. Every muscle is deeply relaxed.*

*A feeling of calmness and contentment washes over you... you are only aware of your own deep relaxation at this time... and you continue to drift into a warm, contented sleep. ...And as you sleep, you drift into another world. This is a beautiful world where there is only happiness and ease and everyone you meet is kind and gentle...*

At this point, you may recite an invocation, such as one of those provided in *Chapter 8*, or simply say, "We now begin this session."

Always close sessions by thanking the spirits for coming and, at least, attempting to communicate with you.

After your session is completed and you turn the lights back on in the room, members of your mediumship development group should each discuss their own impressions of the session and what they felt, heard or saw.

If you received impressions that other people did not,

this does not mean your experience was not an authentic spirit communication. But, if other people experienced similar sights, sounds and sensations, then you have some sense of confirmation.

Keeping a written record of the events and impressions at each session and who was in attendance will help you chart the progress of your mediumship development group.

# CHAPTER 7
# TYPES OF SPIRIT COMMUNICATION

Usually, mediums develop through practice. Initial attempts by new mediums may be weak, but grow stronger with practice. Although, some people are very naturally inclined to communication with spirits and discover their abilities spontaneously.

While these experiences often occur outside the formal setting of a séance, the purpose of the séance is to intentionally provide the spirits with the type of environment and energy they need to perform. Mediumistic talents vary, so séances may include some combination of the following types of communications.

**Clairsentience (the ability to feel the presence of spirits):** The medium and the sitters may feel the presence of a spirit nearby. This is often the first thing that occurs in an instance of spirit communication.

You may experience a sense of electricity in the air or static electricity around yourself. You may suddenly become chilled, as if the temperature has suddenly dropped, which often signals the presence of spirits.

Another aspect of clairsentience is experiencing emotions that are not your own, but are the result of signals you are receiving from spirits.

**Clairaudience (the ability to hear spirits):** Often, a medium and the sitters will hear sounds or voices. These sounds may be very loud and densely physical in nature or softer and more subtle.

When you first begin receiving messages from spirits by this means, you may have trouble distinguishing them from your own inner monologue. When words or ideas begin to come into your head that you do not recognize as your own, this is an indication that you are receiving messages from an external source. With practice, you will begin to immediately recognize when you are receiving messages from a spirit.

If possible, try to confirm whatever information you have received. This might be possible if you have been told something about someone present at the séance, which is known only to that person or about a newsworthy event or a matter that would be the subject of a public record.

**Clairvoyance (the ability to see spirits):** The medium and the sitters may experience visions or see apparitions. These can be visions that appear almost as if on a television screen, they may be vague or distinct.

The vision may be accompanied by specific emotions or other information about the spirit. For example, the spirit of a departed relative may come and stand at the side of one of the sitters and while you receive an impression of how this person looks, you may also pick up on their emotional state or some other aspect about their character. Sometimes spirits are there out of their own curiosity or they have come to visit a living relative whom they care about.

**Channeling:** Channeling or trance mediumship is a state in which the medium's own consciousness has fallen into a passive state in order to permit a spirit to use her life force energy to speak and manifest. Sometimes the medium's voice will change during such a session or an ectoplasm will form over her face giving her the appearance of the spirit who is speaking. This latter phenomenon is called "transfiguration," although the medium's own face is unchanged and can still be discerned behind the superimposed ectoplasm.

The sitters may experience "cold spots" as their own energy as well a that of the medium is consumed in the process of manifestation.

When you first begin channeling, it is important to give free rein to your imagination. As soon as an image or sounds enter your mind, begin giving a voice to what you are seeing and hearing. Silently, invite the spirit to use your energy. They will hear you and once they have your permission, they will begin using you as an instrument.

Allow this happen, even if it seems strange at first or you feel that you're just imagining things. Experience will tell you whether or not these are authentic spirit communications.

Thoughts, images and ideas far removed from your own are excellent indicators that you are experiencing genuine spirit communication.

**Physical Mediumship:** The least common types of physical mediumship involve manifestations of objects and the physical bodies of departed spirits. It, also, includes the ability to move objects, such as table tilting and the production of ethereal sounds such as rapping, footsteps and slamming doors.

The founder of the Spiritists, Allen Kardec, called the manifestation of a physical spirit who can shake hands with and communicate with all of the sitters the

"Perispirit." Its appearance is possible through the production of ectoplasm, which is a concentrated formation of the mediums own bioplasmic energy. Sometimes a cord can be seen, similar to an umbilical cord, running between the body of the medium and the physical manifestation.

Another type of physical mediumship involves the appearance of objects or gifts.

The most common type of physical mediumship involves written communication, either with a pen, through "inspiration" on your computer keyboard, through the use of an old-fashioned writing planchette or a Ouija or spirit board.

## Automatic Writing

Before the invention of the spirit board, early Spiritualists developed a device called the "automatic writing planchette." It resembles the familiar heart-shaped planchette that comes with the classic Ouija board except that it has a small hole drilled near the point and is fitted with a pen or pencil. Like the spirit board, it is usually used in sessions involving more than one sitter, but it has some drawbacks. It can be cumbersome to use and requires copious sheets of paper.

For a single sitter it is more practical to simply sit comfortably at a desk or table with a pad of paper and a pen in hand. Alternatively, you may sit comfortably at your computer with your fingers lightly resting on the keyboard.

As with all spirit communication, it is very important to choose a time and place where you are able to work uninterrupted for an extended period of time. You need time to get sufficiently calm, get your mind quiet and, in case your efforts are successful, you need plenty of time for the communication to take place.

To succeed at automatic writing, you must quiet any nagging worries you have and set them aside for the duration of the sitting. Then, formulate your intention to receive communication, either silently or aloud. Once this is done, empty your mind of all active thought and become entirely receptive to whatever flows through you.

Enter a hypnotic state during the course of your session which may become deeper as you remain in it. Use autosuggestion to help yourself go into this state. Say to yourself, "Whenever I sit in this place with my pen, I am open and ready to receive messages from the spirit world. I am automatically relaxed, my mind becomes quiet and receptive."

You may evoke your Holy Guardian Angel or a spirit with whom you wish to make contact by saying, "In the name of the Most High, I ask my guardian angel to send _____ or some other good spirit to kindly assist me and to keep away any troublesome spirits."

Do not focus on your hands, but let them become passive and willing instruments while your mind remains like a blank slate.

When you begin receiving messages, write them down without analysis. Let the entire transmission be received before you begin to examine it.

During automatic writing, your hands and your pen become instruments for the spirits to use. Some mediums become so adept at receiving transmissions this way that they can receive them through other than their dominant hand and while engaging in other activities. Automatic writing transmissions frequently look nothing like the medium's own penmanship. Some mediums believe that authors who have passed on are actually doing the writing.

Many writers, who do not regard themselves as mediums, often feel as if some spirit or outside force is influencing their writing. A similar kind of effect is felt by musicians and artists and during highly mentally focused states, they are able to produce work that is far beyond their ordinary abilities.

It is impossible to know how many books have been written through automatic writing, but it is safe to assume that many books have been produced this way. Some famous automatic writing transmissions include Jane Robert's communications with an entity named Seth, which resulted a large number of metaphysical books. Pearl Lenore Curran received transmissions from a spirit she called Patience Worth, who claimed to be the spirit of a seventeenth-century Englishwoman. And, Stella Horrocks, who has written numerous books, claims to receive transmission from a few hundred spirits of deceased authors.

Automatic writing is similar to the creative act of writing itself because it involves getting in touch with one's own spirit, which Crowley called the Holy Guardian Angel and the Kabbalists called Silent Self. Transmissions that are outside the scope of the medium's own knowledge, experiences or natural abilities are probably genuine spirit communications.

Interestingly, when people do automatic writing they do not usually perform any ritual, invocation or other elaborate procedure. Nor, is the practice of automatic writing fraught with concerns about demonic possession, which is common with Ouija boards. Although, there is little difference between these two methods of spirit communication.

# CHAPTER 8
# HOW TO USE A OUIJA OR SPIRIT BOARD TO TALK TO THE DEAD

When used correctly, the spirit board is not a toy or a game, but a tool for spiritual development and psychical research.

"Ouija" is Parker Brothers' brand name for the spirit board, which is also sometimes called a talking board or a witch board. While all spirit boards are commonly referred to as Ouija boards, other spirit board manufacturers carefully avoid the term in order to avoid trademark infringement.

The first commercial spirit boards were designed by William Fuld in the United States in the late 19th century. They were constructed entirely of painted and varnished wood, with the familiar arrangement of words, letters and numbers. The word "Yes" was situated in one upper corner, and "No," was in the other. The letters of the alphabet and the numbers from 0 to 9 were, also, placed in rows in the center of the board. Early boards were decorated with symbols that suggested polarity, protection and primal energy.

By means of the planchette (French for "little plank"), which is also called a pointer, indicator or traveler, a spirit can communicate by pointing to letters, numbers or words on the board. The planchette typically has three felt-covered feet, enabling it to move and slide about on the board with ease.

Most modern, mass-manufactured spirit boards are made of cardboard and the planchettes are made of plastic. Some fine wooden spirit boards and planchettes are still being crafted by smaller manufacturers and artists. A good spirit board is made of solid materials and should be large enough for the planchette to slide over letters and numbers without falling off.

Some Ouija historians have said that the spirit board is of ancient origin. It is true that the concept of receiving automatic communications from spirits is likely very old, however, there is no evidence for the Ouija or any other spirit board being any older than the late 19th century.

The spirit board was the logical progression in a series of scientific experiments conducted by Spiritualist investigators, which began in the early part of the 19th century with table tapping, table tipping and the use of automatic writing planchettes. The spirit board was seen by some as a wireless telegraph machine for spirits.

## Reasons to Use a Spirit Board

There are many legitimate uses for spirit boards and few ways to abuse them. As long as the people using the boards are not suffering from mental illness or do not intend harm in some way, there is no danger in using a spirit board.

Most of the fear mongering about spirit boards comes from people who are superstitious, under the influence of fundamentalist religious cults or who have watched too many horror movies and are unable to separate entertainment from facts.

The following are examples of good reasons to use a spirit board:

1. To research and inquire into the nature of life after death.

2. To discover the circumstances of a haunting

3. To communicate with a particular person, such as a departed friend or relative

4. To discover information or gain knowledge regarding a particular subject that can be obtained by no other practical means. For example: Questions about, science, medicine or history.

## Preparation for a Sitting

Obtain a Ouija or spirit board that is in good condition. Spirit boards should be carefully stored away from moisture, extremes of temperature and dust. Wood boards can be waxed for greater ease of movement and velocity of the planchette. Wipe the surface of your spirit board with a soft, clean cloth before each use.

A planchette with three feet is preferable to one with a simple flat bottom because this more traditional style of planchette reduces friction. The felt feet of the planchette should be kept free of dust and lint.

You may place the board on a table or rest it on the participants knees as they sit facing each other. The purpose of placing the board on the operators laps is to increase the buildup of bioplasmic energy in the board.

Begin each fresh attempt by placing the planchette in a blank area in the middle of the board. Always use a light touch with your fingers on the planchette and, of course, do not intentionally push or pull it.

One sitter, two sitters or more may use the board at the same time, although, two sitters are considered optimal. One or both hands may be placed upon the pointer. If sitters use only one hand, it does not matter if it is the left or right hand.

If there are two or more operators, one person should be chosen to speak with the spirits. State your intention aloud. For example, "We would like to speak to _____."

The mental state of the operators should be open, free of worries and more or less blank.

If you have enough people in attendance, assign one person to do nothing else but write down the letters as they are spelled out on the board. The notes should be deciphered at the end of the session. This allows the operators to work without distraction. Any interference with the process could halt communication.

If possible, run an audio recorder during your session or train a video camera on your board so that you can verify what has transpired. Even if your session appears to have been fruitless, you should review your recordings. Sometimes spirit activity, which was not detected at the time it occurred, shows up in audio recordings or on film.

## The Setting

Choose a quiet place where there are no distractions and where you will be able to free your mind from worldly cares and mental preoccupations for the duration of the sitting. Create an atmosphere conducive to total relaxation. For your first session, try sitting in a semi-darkened room, which is sufficiently warm or cool to your liking. You may want to light a candle or burn incense to help create a more meditative environment.

Generally, there is no need to conduct your session in a specific place for it to be successful as long as you can focus your attention on your subject, however, there are exceptions. For example, you might go to a particular location when you are trying to learn about some aspect of its history or in cases where a spirit seems to be confined to a particular place.

The cemetery is not usually a good place to conduct a session because it is not comfortable and you risk exposing your spirit board and other equipment to the elements. Also, cemeteries cause some people to feel depressed or despondent, which might be counterproductive to a positive session. Although, the cemetery can still be a good location if it is appropriate to the particular purpose of your session.

In most cases, whether or not you contact a spirit has more to do with the physical, mental and emotional state of the people at your sitting than it does your location.

## Invocations

Whether you are using the spirit board with others or alone, it is helpful to use an invocation because it signals the sitter(s) and the spirits that a session has begun. You can say something very simple to begin the session, such as "Now, we begin," or you can use a more elaborate invocation.

Depending on your personal preferences, you might try one of the following examples or modify them to come up with something of your own.

## A Wiccan Invocation to the Elements

We call upon the Four Elements and the Watchtowers to oversee this operation.

We open this circle as a consecrated place of love and knowledge.

Guardians of the Watchtowers of the East, share your wisdom with us.

Guardians of the Watchtowers of the South, bring us love, harmony and goodness.

Guardians of the Watchtowers of the West, give us your protection.

Guardians of the Watchtowers of the North, fulfill our needs.

By the power of Air, Fire, Water and Earth, bless this circle and all who stand within it.

By the power of three times three, so mote it be!

## A Wiccan Invocation to the God and Goddess

Goddess, Mother of All, protect me.

God, Father of All, protect me.

Because of you, I am never alone and I am always safe.

I call upon my guardians and guides.

I call upon all of the Forces of Light to join me in this circle.

I seek knowledge and wisdom. Let me be open to receive it.

So mote it be!

## A Prayer

O God, I release my mind to receive the energy of the universe. I desire only that which is good so that I may learn and develop in The Lord's Name. Surround me with the power of the Holy Ghost and protect me with your love. Amen.

## Spiritualist Séance Invocation
## (from *The Spirit Speaks! Weekly Newspaper* 1901)

There is a land where we all go,
whence ne'er the frost nor the cold wind blow,
And friends remembered reunite,
And those who hate, forget their spite,
In glow surround these gentle beings,
We call you now to bless our meetings,
heaven's promise, our spirits thrive
So now for the living, let the dead come alive
Greeting spirits,
Speak thee to us?

## How to Converse with Spirits

There is an often quoted and misunderstood statement made by Aleister Crowley in *Liber al vel Legis 1:57*: "Love is the law; love under will." This statement is an expression of an esoteric scientific principle that is relevant to spirit communication as well as other occult procedures.

Love, in this case, is to be interpreted as harmony or resonance. In order to make contact, you must find resonance with a spirit. This resonant energy then must be directed by your will to communicate.

In order to find resonance with the spirit who is the subject of your query, you must attune your mind to him or her to the exclusion of all else. In this case, you might conduct your session at the home of the departed. Or, you might have an article of clothing, a photograph or something with the departed person's signature on it at the sitting to facilitate a mental and energetic connection.

Focus all your energy on your subject and the matter at hand. When your mind is sufficiently quieted, state your intention aloud: "I wish to speak with _____."

When you make contact with a spirit, always ask for his or her name before proceeding with your conversation.

Some spirit board users consecrate a board for the purpose of contacting just one particular spirit. For example, if you wanted to use your spirit board to communicate with only your deceased aunt, then you would state that intention and never use that board to contact any other spirit.

As you continue to conduct regular sessions, you may encounter the same one or more spirits repeatedly. These spirits, called controls, may assist you by locating other spirits and facilitating communication with them. After you are comfortable with a particular spirit, call him or her by name at the beginning of a session.

Once you are in contact with a spirit, you must be prepared to carry on a conversation. In order to not break the flow, it is a good idea to have a list of pre-determined questions ready. You may end up not using any of them, but you will have some ideas ready in case you need them.

Always be polite when addressing a spirit, just as you would if you were conversing with a living person.

**Examples of questions to ask the spirit:**

1. What is your name?
2. Where do you come from?
3. Are you a good spirit?
4. Where do you live now?
5. What do you do?
6. Do you have something you would like to tell us?

In the spirit of inquiry, it is reasonable to ask polite questions about almost anything. For example: The nature of other worlds; the past; the future; the location of lost items or about the spirit's past life.

## How to Have a Pleasant Session with the Spirit Board

Critics say that spirit boards are dangerous because they represent an open invitation to any spirit whatsoever, some of whom are malevolent. They say the boards can become a doorway through which dangerous or unpleasant entities can enter. This may be true, but the board itself has no power; it depends entirely on the operators, which is why you must be mindful of your thoughts and emotions at a sitting.

If you go into a session looking for mischief, you could have an unpleasant experience. Therefore, do not enter into a spirit board session with the object of seeking cheap thrills and do not sit with people who are not serious-minded. If for no other reason, it is pointless to do so.

If you or anyone who is participating becomes frightened or anxious, end the session immediately. If that person is frequently or easily frightened, do not sit with him or her because fear is an invitation to unpleasant spirits.

If you have undesirable or unpleasant or

communications with a spirit, simply break the connection with the entity by taking your hands off the planchette. This is the equivalent of hanging up on an obscene telephone caller.

The principle of resonance applies when you ask, "Is there anyone here who would like to speak with us?" Therefore, as you ask this question, keep your focus on the positive. If you are not attempting to contact a specific spirit by name, invite one who is knowledgeable about something you would like to discuss.

**Remember:** Where you direct your mind, the condition of your emotions and, essentially, what kind of person you are will determine the kind of experience you have with the spirit board.

## How Does the Spirit Board Work?

Some people believe the spirit board works through unconscious muscular action on the part of the operators. But, this explanation cannot account for all of the experiences that spirit board users have. For instance, at times, the planchette can be seen moving around on the board, spelling out letters for a few seconds after the sitters have removed their hands from it.

The explanation for this occurrence is the absorption into the device of psychokinetic (PK) energy from the bioplasmic fields of the sitters. This energy is infused into the planchette so that it becomes a medium, which the spirits can use to interact with those on the physical plane of existence.

Spirits seem to be able to recognize those among the living who are willing and able to make contact with them. When questioned, some spirits have said that they were attracted to the energy or "the light" of the people at the sitting.

## What to Do If the Planchette Does Not Respond Properly

Sometimes it takes a little while before the planchette begins to move. This is because sufficient psychokinetic energy must be build up in it. Therefore, you may have to work regularly with the board for a while before you obtain the desired results.

In order to manifest, spirits require sitters who are in good health and have a strong life force energy. Give the spirits permission to use your bioplasmic force by saying, "I give you permission to use my energy so you can communicate."

Some people are naturally more endowed with a personal supply of energy than others. If you have more than two people working with the board, experiment with different combinations of operators. For example, choose two people who are polar opposites. This doesn't necessarily mean two people of different genders, but who bring different elements to the sitting. For example, if you have one person who is particularly vivacious and energetic and another who is particularly psychically sensitive and receptive, these two people might make the best partners.

If you have been sitting for ten minutes and the planchette is still not moving, try getting it going by gently guiding it on the board in a figure "8" pattern. This technique is intended to help build up the kinetic energy of the spirit board.

If that doesn't work, take a break for 15 minutes or so while you enjoy a light, natural snack and drink plenty of water.

Whenever you are not obtaining good results, try to keep your sessions to about half an hour. Anything more and you're likely to become tired and drained, which will make you of little use to the process.

If your planchette is moving, but you are receiving irrelevant messages or gibberish, this may be a sign that more than one spirit is struggling for access to the sitting. Be patient and stay focused. Continue to record the communication because the transmission may make more sense to you after you have time to closely examine it.

## Test Your Abilities

One way to test your abilities is to sit at the board blindfolded and see if you still receive coherent messages. This exercise will remove any doubt about the role of any conscious or unconscious pushing of the planchette or the question of chicanery on the part of the sitters.

In her book, *Voices from the Void, Six Years Experience in Automatic Communications*, published in 1919, Hester Travers Smith describes spirit communications received while the participants, including Mrs. Smith were blindfolded.

The following script from this work is illustrative of how to – and perhaps how not to – speak with a spirit:

**Question:** (For whom is this message?)
**Answer:** Everybody.
**Question:** (Spell your name.)
**Answer:** Alice Franks.
**Question:** (Can't you work quicker?)
**Answer:** No.
**Question:** (Go on, please.)
**Answer:** Your overbearing attitude will not make me go any faster. I lived and died at... Upper Norwood.
**Question:** (Did you die recently?)
**Answer:** Yes.
**Question:** (What date?)

**Answer:** I was unconscious for many days; I believe that I passed over between Friday and yesterday morning.

**Question:** (Have you anything special to say?)

**Answer:** My pain was intense, and I am still in pain. Good-bye."

Such an experiment can now be easily made by even a single person using a video camera to tape the session. As always, if you receive any information about a person or event at your sittings, try to verify it by conventional means.

## Closing a Session

When the spirits have ceased communications, when the sitters are tired or the sitting has reached the end of its appointed time, formally close the session.

You may close by simply saying, "Thank you for talking with us. We're going, now. Good bye!"

If you opened your session with a Wiccan invocation, you may close in a similar fashion by addressing the Four Elements or the God and Goddess and saying, "Thank you for blessing our circle, now we bid you go in peace."

Another way to close is with a prayer: "Thank you for the wisdom and insight, which you have granted us. Protect this house and the people in it. In the name of God, we thank you. Amen."

Snuffing out a candle you lit at the beginning of the session or ringing a bell are other ways to signal an end to the proceedings.

Communication with spirits using a spirit board can be a relaxing and life-enhancing exercise, which you can enjoy alone or with friends. It is a good tool for meditation and it represents an opportunity to make your own scientific inquiry into the nature of the world.

You will get out of the spirit board whatever you put into it. When you approach it with an open mind and good intentions, you will benefit from the knowledge you receive and enjoy increased psychic sensitivity.

# CHAPTER 9
# SPIRIT COMMUNICATION THROUGH ELECTRONIC DEVICES

Early interest in spirit communication grew rapidly as new technology, such as the wireless telegraph, phonograph and radio, was introduced to the public in the 19th century. A connection between the new science of electricity, magnetism, waves and frequencies was made to explain spirit communication. Inventors designed machines to assist mediums at séances, such as the Spiritual Telegraph Dial, which was invented by Mr. J. T. Pease in about 1854. At the time of his death in 1931, Thomas Edison was still at work on an electronic device that would assist Spiritualists in their inquiries into the existence of life after death.

By the 1960s there was a resurgence of interest in E.S.P., characterized by academic and scientific inquiry into the nature of life after death. Researchers like George Meek of the MetaScience Foundation of North

Carolina, who invented the SpiriCom device, Franz Seidl of Austria, who invented the Psycho Phone II, and numerous others continued the quest of the early 19th century Spiritualist pioneers to design an electronic device with which to reliably communicate with spirits in real time.

Instrumental Trans-Communication is the term applied to the employment of electronic devices, such as audio recorders, telephones, television sets, computers and radios, to act as a medium through which spirits can communicate with the living.

Audio recorders are commonly used to record Electric Voice Phenomena (E.V.P.), but this form of communication is somewhat limiting because the audio must be played back for the voices to be heard. Using an audio recorder for this purpose is much like any other type of spirit communication. Typically, people go to a haunted location, which is free of wind and external noise and chatter, to ask questions of the spirits. Either cassette tape recorders or digital recorders may be used in such experiments, depending on your preference.

When a person's mind is quiet and receptive, spirits sometimes use telephones to communicate in real time. While it is not the most commonly reported type of communication, some people receive phone calls from deceased relatives or other spirits who have an important message for them.

Some people have received communications through the television, particularly by means of analog signals that produce "snow" or static. The static or "white noise" produced by an ordinary radio or even an electric fan has been used by spirits to form their voices and speak to the living. More rarely, people report receiving messages from the spirits of departed friends and relatives on their computer screens.

In many instances of communication through

telephones, televisions or computers, it is the spirits who initiate contact with the living. They may have something important they want to say to a living relative or they have interests in common with the contactee. For example, living people who have an interest in healing have been contacted by the spirits of departed doctors.

Spirits commonly manifest as orbs or more distinct ghostly formations in photographs and videos. They can, also, be seen through the lens of the camera in real time. Very often, if you ask them to do something like pose for a picture or follow you, they will oblige.

Many paranormal researchers believe they have found a way to use radios to tune into a spirit's frequency range and communicate directly with them in real time. A variety of radio-based electronic devices have been developed and continue to be improved upon by an unknown number of independent researchers. Some are based on devices like George Meek and Bill O'Neill's Spiricom and Frank Sumpter's design, which is called the Frank's Box or the Ghost Box.

Most of these devices are essentially modified radios that produce white noise or an electronic hum, which spirits can manipulate to form audible words. Some of them resemble radionics computers and similarly they must be tuned by a psychically sensitive person. Plans for such devices are scattered around the web along with videos of people using them. Search online for "Frank's Box Plans" or "Ghost Box Plans," to see how these devices are constructed. Information about the Spiricom and other devices is available at WorldITC (www.worlditc.com).

Whenever you use battery-powered electronic devices for spirit communication, keep extra batteries on hand because spirit manifestations often rapidly drain the batteries in such devices.

Using electronic devices to communicate with spirits

is very similar to previously discussed methods. Once you are aware of a spirit's presence and willingness to communicate with you, address him or her as you would if you were at a classical séance or using a spirit board.

# CHAPTER 10
# THE DUMB SUPPER

The dumb supper is another method of spirit communication, which is similar to the séance. It is called a "dumb" supper because it is conducted in complete silence. It is performed to contact the spirits of friends and family members who have passed on and historically by young women to summon the spirits of their future husbands.

Traditionally, it is performed on or around Halloween to honor ancestors, but like other forms of spirit communication or ritual, it can be done at any time and it is most effective when it is performed on a regular schedule at the same hour on the same day of the week.

Set an appointment for your dumb supper at midnight or later. You may begin by sweeping the floors in your kitchen and dining room to physically and spiritually cleanse the area. Then, turn off all electric lighting and light one or two candles and place them on the table or use old-fashioned kerosene lamps to dimly illuminate the room.

A dumb supper can be conducted alone or with two or three other people. If you are working with others, divide the tasks of cooking and setting the table for yourselves and your guests.

The meal you prepare can be as simple or elaborate as you like. If the purpose of your dumb supper is to invite the spirits of friends and family members who have passed on, choose a menu that includes their favorite dishes. You may, also, place photographs or items that belonged to the person on the table near their plates.

In the Ozark Mountain region, it is customary to serve a simple meal of sweet corn bread with butter (recipe below). Alternatively, you may serve any sort of meal you like in one or more courses. If you serve multiple courses, do so in reverse order. For example, serve dessert first, then the main course followed by the appetizer.

If you are working with other people, take turns stirring, cooking and baking without uttering a sound. Do as many things in reverse as possible and in total silence. For example, add ingredients to the bowl in reverse order and stir the batter in a counter-clockwise direction.

Set the table with a chair, plate, glass, set of utensils and a napkin for each living guest and each expected spirit guest. The entire process of setting the table must be done in reverse. Items on the table should be arranged opposite to where they would normally be placed. Walk backwards as you distribute the plates, glasses, napkins, silverware, butter, salt and pepper shakers and condiments. If you are right-handed, set the table with your left hand and vice versa. Place forks on the right and knives and spoons on the left. Place glasses at the upper left corner of the plate.

Once the table is set and the meal is prepared, serve it in silence and in the most solemn and respectful manner. Each living guest may prepare an individual prayer ahead of time, which is to be placed beneath the plate of the anticipated spirit guest. Optionally, you may open the doors and windows to invite the spirits in. Then, sit at your own place at the table. Bow your head reverently and silently call upon the spirits to join you at the table.

The spirits may take their seat at the table any time during the course of the meal or they may make some other sign of their presence. Before spirits arrive, you may hear the howling of dogs or the shrieking of birds. Objects may materialize on the table and other manifestations of spirit communication, similar to those associated with séances, may occur.

There are many variations on this ritual which is very old and appears in different regions of the United States. In some accounts, nine different objects must be laid upon the table, which include the prepared dishes and condiments. Sometimes as soon as the table is set, the lights are all extinguished except for small black candles, which are placed directly on the plates of the spirit guests.

## Sweet Corn Bread Recipe

### Ingredients:

1 cup white flour
1 cup yellow cornmeal
1/3 cup white sugar
1/3 cup brown sugar
1 tsp. sea salt
3 1/2 tsp. baking powder
1 egg
1 cup milk
1/3 cup vegetable oil

### Directions:

Preheat oven to 400 degrees F (200 degrees C). In a large bowl, combine the above dry ingredients and blend them. Then, stir in the egg, milk and oil. Blend this batter until it is free of large lumps. Pour it into a greased 11" x 7" baking dish.

Bake at 400 degrees for 20 to 25 minutes or until a toothpick inserted into the middle comes out clean. Cut it into little golden squares and serve with butter.

# CHAPTER 11
# SUMMONING ANGELS AND DEMONS

According to ancient Hebrew lore, the natural order of things on this planet is that human beings have dominion over the angels. An ancient war between the angels ensued when one faction refused to subordinate themselves to human beings, whom they regard as inferior. These angels became known as the fallen ones or demons.

*The Emerald Tablets of Thoth*, translated by Dr. Doreal and around which the Brotherhood of the White Temple was created, tells a similar story of entities who dwell in the dark places in the earth in another dimension and who are constantly trying to come back into this one by tricking magicians into conjuring them and allowing themselves to become possessed by them.

Many people avoid contact with or knowledge of demons because they fear them, however, it is the destiny of mankind to rule over these beings.

Many people do not believe such beings exist. Yet, demonic entities are so numerous that they are unavoidable to psychics who can see and otherwise sense them. Those who are able to see them can sometimes hear their thoughts, also.

The appearance of these beings varies greatly. Some look more or less human, but they are extremely frightening not only because of their appearance but because of their malevolence and hatred of all things beautiful and noble in humanity. To come face to face with them is to confront the very essence of evil and it is an experience that will stay with you for the rest of your life.

They are attracted like flies to scenes involving fear. They sometimes flock to people who have been victims of horrible acts of violence so they can feed on this energy, which is why some conjurers use blood sacrifices or perverted sex acts to draw them.

But, they can be drawn and commanded without these things. Furthermore, they are cowards at heart and they are terribly afraid of the psychics who can see them. A great deal of the power they wield over mankind exists because they are hidden from sight and so many people do not believe they exist. It would be nice to think that there are no such things as horrible and evil as this, but the fact is they exist hidden among the living as well as in the spirit realm and they are plentiful.

Many people who see them will not openly admit it. This is partly because demonic entities are so horrifying and anomalous in appearance that their minds simply edit them out: "No! I didn't just see that." Furthermore, seeing demons or hearing demonic voices is associated with schizophrenia and other serious mental disorders. So, there is a natural tendency for many people to go into denial when they have such experiences and even those who do acknowledge what they have seen are prudently reluctant to talk about it.

Demonic entities operate on a very densely physical electronic frequency near our own, which can be detected in the high range of an ordinary EMF (Electromagnetic Frequency) detector like those used by electricians. Not only are they attracted to these frequencies, but they can sometimes produce them in instances where there is no apparent source for such a high electromagnetic field. This is why many people experience headaches, breathing difficulties and weakness during encounters with them. They can, also, produce a sulphurous smell similar to that of rotten eggs.

Their greatest enemies are the archangels who are very large, intimidating beings that radiate a silvery light. They are extremely powerful and antagonistic toward the fallen ones, however, they must be called upon for assistance because they have a policy of non-interference in human affairs unless permission is expressly granted.

There are other angelic beings who are not necessarily warriors like the archangels, but who can be called upon in times of distress. For example, if you or someone else is ill or in need of comfort, they will help you in tangible ways. They do not seem to be as near our vibratory plane. Their manifestations are palpable, but far less physical than those of the demons, which can be very densely physical.

The angels, who are all light-radiating beings regardless of their individual features, are able to do miraculous things for people who call upon them. They are frequently credited with saving lives in real, physical ways. For example, there have been instances where people trapped in burning vehicles suddenly found themselves safely outside their cars through some remarkable means.

Angels may be called upon silently or aloud. You must find resonance with them and direct your will to communicate, just as you would in your attempts to contact any other spirit.

All angels of light are powerful, however, if you are in a confrontation with demonic entities, the archangels have the most power to constrain them. If you are in a situation of great distress, are under psychic attack or you want to summon a demon for some purpose, it is beneficial to invoke the archangels for assistance. They will help protect you from demonically possessed people, too.

Along with the archangels, there are certain words, names or aspects of "god" that you can use to compel demonic entities to behave in certain ways, which are commonly used in formal conjurations.

There is no clear answer as to why any of this is so, except that this planet is very old and it is likely that innumerable dramas have occurred in the past and some are still being played out between a variety of actors.

## Ceremonial Magic

In centuries past, the study of angels and demons was part of the science of alchemy. Like their later Spiritualist counterparts, the early alchemists kept records of their experiments and worked to perfect their techniques.

There have always been questions about which of these spirits are truly angels and which are demons. All of them, including the dark spirits, may be referred to as angels. Attempts by magicians to communicate with such beings in the past resulted in skepticism about the nature of the beings and persecution.

The level of caution with which you approach the

summoning of any of these beings is a matter of your own discretion. If you are afraid of any of it, you should refrain completely. But, demonic entities cannot enter the body of a physically and mentally sound person unless they are invited or they find a weakness they can exploit.

People who take working with spirits seriously usually refrain from the use of alcohol and drugs, which can leave you open to obsession or possession. Many street drugs and the class of drugs provided to people diagnosed with depression or other mental illnesses leave people vulnerable to dark entities.

Dark entity attachments can cause poor health, draining of the life force, fatigue, anxiety, misfortune and madness. Some entities prompt people to commit dangerous or evil acts; some even set up their hosts so they are caught and punished.

Practicing vegetarianism even just for a period of days before a summoning can make contact easier. Some magicians from antiquity fasted in preparation for summoning rituals. Refraining from eating heavy earthy food slightly raises your vibratory rate so you can more easily see and communicate with the angels, in particular, the fallen ones who are closer to our own vibratory range.

In your early efforts, attempt to make contact with angels or demons who have a reputation for having a good nature and a desire to help humanity. Examples from *The Lesser Key of Solomon* are: King Purson, Prince Vassago, Duke Elligos, Count Morax, Count Ipos, Marquis Forneus, and Duke Alloces.

**King Purson:** Taking a human or aerial body, he answers truly of all secret and divine things of Earth and the creation of the world. He also brings good familiars.

**Prince Vassago:** He can be persuaded to tell the magician of events past and future, can discover hidden and lost things, and has a good nature. Many white witches and diviners are especially partial to him.

**Duke Elligos:** He discovers hidden things and knows the future of wars and attracts the favor of lords, knights and other important persons.

**Count Morax:** He teaches astronomy and all other liberal sciences and gives the magician good and wise familiars who know the virtues of all herbs and precious stones.

**Count Ipos:** He knows and can reveal all things, past, present and future and he can make men witty and valiant.

**Marquis Forneus:** He teaches eloquent oratory and languages, endows the magician with a good reputation and causes him to be loved by both friends and enemies.

**Duke Alloces:** He induces people to immorality and teaches arts and all mysteries of the sky.

Another helpful and benign spirit to make contact with is, Lucifer, a Promethean advocate for mankind who is interested in human empowerment and is in no way dangerous. He may be called upon for spiritual enlightenment and education in all matters. Lucifer is not the same being as Satan, who is the adversary of mankind according to the Christian *Bible* (*New Testament*).

Consult the *Lesser Key of Solomon* or other grimoires to determine which spirit you would like to contact.

Each entity has specific characteristics. Note that each angel and demon has his own sigil (symbol), which is an energy pattern. It acts an antenna to draw the particular entity. Make a photocopy of these images or trace them on a plain piece of paper for use in your summoning. Many sources for such sigils are in the public domain.

### The following is a list of popular grimoires:

*The Goetia or The Lesser Key of Solomon*
*The Grimoire of Turiel*
*The Grimoire of Honorius*
*The Grimoirum Verum*
*John Dee's Grimoirium Imperium*
*The Necronomicon*
*Verus Jesuitarum Libellus*

In these grimoires you will find powerful conjurations for summoning dark entities. These vary and you may have to experiment a while to determine which ones work best for you. You may use your own wording, but there is no point in reinventing the wheel when past researchers have already done a lot of the work for you. Furthermore, there is a powerful energy imprint in formal prayers or invocations in the old grimoires. Whatever invocation you choose, let it be one that stirs great emotion in you. Your strong emotions will give even more power the words.

Some grimoires give advice with regard to astrological timing. These are only starting points for your experiments, however, and performing your ritual at that exact time does not guarantee success. Nonetheless, take note of the timing and other external factors, as discussed in *Chapter 13*, just as you would for other kinds of paranormal research. In your own experiments you may find that certain hours of the day, positions of the stars and phases of the moon make contact much easier or render it nearly impossible.

As with other methods of spirit communication, it is ideal to set a side a time and day of the week for your work and perform it regularly.

Ideally, you should have a place outside where you can do the ritual without being disturbed. Otherwise, you will need a sufficiently large room. Some people object to summoning dark entities into their homes but, of course, this is a matter of personal comfort.

Whenever you conjure powerful, dark entities, surround yourself and anyone you are working with in a circle drawn both for protection and to focus energy. The entity should be summoned into a triangle, placed just outside the circle.

The circle should be nine feet in diameter. Two feet away from it, draw a triangle with equal sides of three feet each. If you are working inside, you may use masking tape to mark off the location for the circle and triangle. Some modern magicians like to place the triangle to the north of the circle, but because of the energetic flow of the earth, you may be more successful if you place it in the east.

Place a reflective object within the triangle. A large quartz crystal, a black scrying mirror or a bowl of water are often used. If you fail to produce a full physical manifestation, you may be able to see the image of the demon in the reflection. Also, within the triangle, place the sigil associated with the entity you intend to conjure.

It is very important that once the ritual is underway that no one steps or reaches outside the circle, which is an energy vortex and psychic barrier. This is especially critical when you are dealing with malefic dark entities who are especially hostile to humans like, for example, Marquis Andras of the *Goetia*. It is said that these entities will devour the magician, however, in practice what happens most often is they will drain the person's life force very quickly and the person may go numb in parts of their body or lose consciousness.

The Lesser Banishing Ritual of the Pentagram, which is given in Israel Regardie's *The Golden Dawn*, is one of the most elegant procedures for calling a circle of protection by the archangels. Before you use this ritual, you should be able to recite the words with passion and go through all the steps and visualizations by rote and without hesitation.

It is worth mentioning that for people who are very familiar with ceremonial magic that it is possible to summon demonic entities from the grimoires by mentally going through the rituals. The spirits can be instructed and you can receive messages from them in a light trance state. This works well for communicating with and dispatching low level entities, such as familiars, to perform tasks for you, too.

A mostly a mental method of summoning demonic entities is given in the Necronomicon Spell Book. It allows you to summon the entities without the expenditure of time and the tedium of learning ceremonial magic. No circle of protection is used. The entire procedure is done mentally through visualization, while you are in a trance state.

Keep in mind that the Simon *Necronomicon*, itself, appears to be designed to infect readers with dark entities. In his book, *The Grimoire of the Necronomicon,* Donald Tyson states that the Simon *Necronomicon*, although it is obviously not all it claims, nonetheless, seems to have a very real spell or curse placed on it. While there are some obvious inconsistencies in the book's narrative, the entities represented by the symbols in it seem to have real power.

Even after silently reading the *Necronomicon* you may find yourself plagued by shadowy annoyances scampering around inside your home, which may require you to do a cleansing. These are low level entities, which are little shadowy imps, but they should not be allowed to go out of control. At the very least, they are annoying and there is a story about a man's house catching on fire from allowing these creatures to run about the house unchecked. Sometimes they can simply be ordered away if you speak aggressively to them. Simply saying, "Get out!" can be effective.

The *Grimoirium Imperium* by John Dee is a powerful document for summoning dubious angelic entities. The book cautions the reader that even reading it silently can cause unwholesome entities to appear and it is recommended that they be conjured within a circle. John Dee and Edward Kelley came up with very elaborate and colorful protocols for constraining these entities.

Extremely powerful conjurations are given in the Jesuits' *Libellus Magicus*. The Jesuits are accomplished at conjuring and controlling these entities. If you use these rites, consider accompanying your ceremony with a soundtrack of Gregorian chanting. Its purpose is to draw the Grigori, who are, at least, 200 demons mentioned in the Biblical *Book of Enoch* who took wives from among human women.

Generally, be firm but polite in your conversations with dark spirits. They are fond of hierarchies and like to believe they are superior to human beings. Remind them of the true order of things whenever it is necessary. Regardless of their titles, you are the true sovereign and their master according to the rules that were set forth long ago. They know this, but many of them hope you do not.

Dealing with these entities is a little like dealing with

a public servant or government clerk. If the ancient Sumerian texts are right, then our systems of government and civilization came from them. In fact, many people who work in hierarchical systems in positions of perceived authority, such as law enforcement agents, judges, lawmakers, customs agents and government employed clerks are governed by dark entities.

The fallen angels are very individual in their appearance and personalities. If they are reluctant to cooperate with you, speak to them as you would a public servant who is trying to overstep the boundaries of his authority. Be polite but firm and remind them of the order of things, which is that they work for you.

If this doesn't work, be firmer by invoking the natural law, which makes you the spirit's master. If that fails, make threats, for example, to confine the spirit inside an object or inflict pain upon it. If those threats fail, then carry them out until the spirit submits to your will.

It is not necessary to make any kinds of deals or pacts with these creatures in which you promise them something that belongs to you. You are their sovereign master; they work for you. They might try to convince you otherwise. But, stand firm.

Whatever method of communication with them you choose, dismiss the entities when your conversation with them is finished, even if you believe your attempt was unsuccessful. If you are conducting a ceremonial ritual, dismiss the spirit, then wait a few minutes before you step outside the circle. In ceremonial magic this final part of the conjuration is called the "License to Depart" and there are many eloquent recitations for the dismissal of spirits from the various grimoires, which you can employ in your rituals.

The following is an ancient procedure for giving

spirits the license to depart: First, burn frankincense on a hot charcoal. Once it has burned, apply a small amount of dried thyme and allow this to burn.

Even if you are using a mental method of contact, once you have finished your discourse, the spirits should be thanked if they were cooperative and asked to go in peace.

# CHAPTER 12
## EXORCISM: GETTING RID OF SPIRITS

Exorcism is the act of getting rid of an unwelcome spirit of any nature. This is done in different ways, depending on the type of spirit concerned.

In the case of the common ghost, which is the spirit of a departed person or animal, just clearing a room of unwholesome or discordant energies by smudging with sage is usually sufficient. To do this, acquire a dried bundle of White Sage from your local metaphysical shop or online store, light the end of it, put out the flame and let it smoke. You may want to use a bowl to catch the ashes as you proceed from room to room, allowing the smoke to drift into each corner.

Similarly, a person who is feeling disturbed or is suffering from a parasitic energy attachment may be relieved of it (sometimes permanently, but other times only temporarily) when the smoke is allowed to drift all around them.

After smudging with sage, summon benevolent, protective spirits by performing the same procedure using the smoke from a braid of sweet grass.

One symptom of a house that is infected with demonic entities is that smudging with sage only makes matters worse. These entities must be dealt with in a different way. Sprinkling blessed salt or Holy Water, obtained from a Catholic Church, around your house and in every corner may calm things down.

If your house is infested by particularly stubborn dark entities, command them to leave in a forceful voice, invoking the name of the leader of the angels of light. They respond to self-righteous anger and the name of Yeshua, which is the inverse of Yod He Vau He or the Tetragrammaton. You do not have to understand or believe in it for it to work. Just address the dark spirits and angrily say, "In the name of Yeshua, the Most High Holy God, I order you to leave this house and never return!"

You may have to be persistent, performing the exorcism a few times before it is clean and re-infestation does not occur.

Call upon Michael the Archangel to cleanse protect your home from all negative entities. Find an image of St. Michael or another powerful-looking angel from a book or a painting. Practice holding this image in your mind by glancing at the picture and then closing your eyes and picturing it in your mind's eye. Repeat this until you have the angelic image firmly in your mind and can recall it at any time.

Then, perform the following mental ritual as you are preparing to go to sleep or any time you need protection:

Imagine Michael the Archangel, dressed in royal red and blue, armed with a great flaming sword, glowing with a powerful light. With your eyes closed, imagine the room you are presently in. Visualize Michael standing behind you and silently ask him to cleanse your house of negative energies.

See him walking through the room, illuminating every corner of it with bright, powerful, cleansing light. Then, one by one, visualize him walking through every room in your house, spreading powerful positive energy and destroying all negativity simply by his presence. Once the angel has cleansed every room in your house, simply tell him, "Thank you!"

The Catholic Church has its own exorcism rites and in the past several years there has been an increase in the number of these performed. For a time, the Catholic Church did not teach priests to perform exorcisms, at all. In fact, many priests, much like many psychologists and ordinary people, did not believe in possession by demons until they were faced with the facts. Although demonic activity is on the rise, the Catholic Church still has relatively few priests who are capable of performing exorcisms. Furthermore, there is some question about the efficacy of their methods.

Among the most powerful rituals for dealing with demonic entities are those with a free masonic foundation like those of The Golden Dawn.

In an article entitled "Spirit Evocation & Exorcism – A New Look at That Old Black Magick," *Fate Magazine*, March 2004, Vol. 57, Number 3, Issue 647, author Lon Milo DuQuette tells how he assisted Israel Regardie of the O.T.O. (Ordo Templis Orientalis) with the ceremonial magic-style exorcism of a woman who was an incest victim, plagued by a dark spirit who had become her childhood protector. As she grew older, the entity grew violent and made her sick and unable to live a normal life.

Regardie performed the ritual with, at least, two other people in support roles, all in full ceremonial regalia. The demon was summoned into a black mirror. Regardie attempted to reason with the spirit, but he refused to comply, so Regardie banished him using Enochian conjurations and the woman was able to go on and lead a normal life.

This was a fortunate case. In some very difficult cases, people have multiple attachments that have to be pulled off in layers through multiple rituals. In such instances, it may take years to fully detach the entities.

Increasingly, nonhuman souls are entering human bodies. Such people are psychopaths who appear human, but have a demonic nature. But, a large percentage of people are "organic portals" who came into the world sharing their body with more than one spirit. Many of these people appear to be sociopaths who do not have ordinary human emotions. There is no known remedy for these conditions.

There are some mental disorders that seem to involve entity attachments and possession, such as schizophrenia and DID (Dissociative Identity Disorder). Some experts believe these victims may benefit from exorcism. Specific cases involving people with these conditions are discussed in the book, *Possession & Exorcism*, by Dr. Hans Naegeli-Osjord, M.D., a pragmatic psychologist who concluded that his patients were possessed by a variety of different types entities.

Some psychic healing practitioners, Hoodoo witch doctors and Mexican curanderos all have special knowledge about demonic entities because they work with them regularly and believe they are the cause of some cases of mental and physical illnesses. Such people may be of assistance in cases of serious demonic possession or obsession.

The book, *Magical Healing: How to Use Your Mind to Heal Yourself and Others*, discusses how to recognize energy attachments and destroy them. Spiritual attachments are like tentacles or cords coming from the spirits of people, either living or dead, which can drain the life force energy and cause emotional disturbances in victims.

With practice, you can sense these attachments with your hands or clairvoyantly see them. You remove them by visualizing them being severed. Then, you balance and heal the person's chakra system. Sometimes if a person is in ill health or experiencing minor emotional disturbances, they will experience immediate relief from this procedure.

While many people shrink from the idea of communicating with spirits, particularly those of a darker nature, it is vital to a fuller understanding of the world around us. Since we are already surrounded by these intelligent energies, there is no reason to fear them.

The skills involved in spirit communication are directly related to other esoteric disciplines, including healing, divination and spell casting. All of these subjects are inter-related and the mastery of one of them aides in the mastery of all the others.

# CHAPTER 13
## EXTERNAL AND ATMOSPHERIC INFLUENCES ON SPIRIT COMMUNICATION

The factors that affect the success or failure of any spirit communication session can be described in terms of three internal ones and large number of external ones. The internal factors are those over which you may have some control while external factors are beyond your control.

The three internal factors required for mediumistic spirit communication are: (1) Good physical health; (2) a strong bioplasmic field; and (3) the ability to attune psychically or resonate with spiritual energy and exercise your will.

The numerous external factors are comprised of atmospheric conditions involving such things as the position of the planets and weather conditions. The phases of the moon, the electromagnetic activity in the earth caused by sunspot activity and planetary alignments are some of the variables known by both ancient and modern researchers to influence the outcome of spirit communication, either positively or negatively.

While the following external factors cannot be controlled and observing them is no assurance of success, it may be beneficial to, at least, consider them in the course of your research:

**The Moon**

The moon has an effect on the tides and our physical bodies. For centuries, it has been known to have an influence on the mind, hence the term "lunatic." In astrology, the location of the moon in your planetary chart that influences the nature of your mind.

Some occult researchers believe that the moon may be an artificial satellite whose position can affect frequencies coming to the earth from outer space. It has long been believed to have an influence on paranormal events. Many paranormal researchers report more spirit activity during the full moon or the new moon. Also, many Spiritualists and other researchers report greater success at night, although spirit communication can occur at any time of day.

## The Sun

Sun flares and geomagnetic storms increase the electricity in the environment making it easier for spirit communication and manifestations to occur.

Interestingly, sun spot activity has been very low in recent years. Some scientists believe this has led to a natural cooling of the earth's temperature, although this conclusion is controversial. Sun spot activity is cyclical.

Check the current activity of the sun at: www.n3kl.org.

## Planetary Influences

Local Sidereal Time (LST) is used by astrologers to keep track of planetary movements. Psychical researchers have found that their experiments render more accurate results at a Local Sidereal Time of 13:30. It is the time of Galactic Center Rising. It is, also, referred to as "Libra Time" because the constellation Libra is at 24 degrees and almost directly overhead.

This conclusion is documented by Dr. James P. Spottiswoode and Edwin C. May in, "Anomalous Cognition Effect Size: Dependence on Sidereal Time and Solar Wind Parameters," in *The Journal for Scientific Exploration*. See this and other documentation at: http://www.jsasoc.com/library.html.

Determine your Local Sidereal Time by using a LST calculator or a sidereal clock. Free smart phone applications and software are now available online for this purpose.

Calculate your Local Sidereal Time using your longitude at: http://tycho.usno.navy.mil/sidereal.html.

## Sabbats

Certain dates may prove more favorable for spirit communication. The following Sabbats or traditional holy days are times when powerful cosmic rays strike the earth. The actual time of each occasion may vary by a day in any given year. Consult an astrological calendar, a Witches' Almanac or a Farmers' Almanac for the precise days and hours.

**Halloween or Samhain:** October 31st
**Yule or Winter Equinox:** December 21st
**Imbolc:** February 2nd
**Ostara or Spring Equinox:** March 21st
**Beltane or May Day:** April 30th
**Litha or Summer Equinox:** June 21st
**Lughnassadh:** August 2nd
**Mabon or Autumn Equinox:** September 21st

## Weather

Some researchers believe that thunderstorms imbue the air with electricity, thus making a better atmosphere for spirits to communicate. But, others report better success when the skies are clear and calm. Both of these external factors, stormy weather and sunny skies, represent variables you can apply to your own experiments.

## How to Document Your Research

Documentation is an important part of successful psychical research. Keep a journal just for this purpose.

The following are examples of details to make note of in your research:

1. Note the date and time when the session began and ended.

2. Note the names of the participants in the session and what they contributed to the session.

3. Note the moon phase.

4. Note weather conditions.

5. Note the planetary phase.

6. Note the solar activity.

7. What equipment was used, ie. audio recorder, video recorder.

8. Whether or not communications were received.

9. What was the exact nature of the communication: What did the spirit say?

10. Any other phenomena that may have accompanied the event, such as poltergeist activity.

11. Impressions, feelings or sensations of the participants.

12. Any other variables that might be of importance.

Angela Kaelin

# GLOSSARY

**Angels:** Beings of light who are helpers to mankind. The are a part of the godhead. The four archangels, Michael (Mi-ki-gal), Gabriel, Raphael and Uriel are the greatest enemies of the demons. Other types of angels include the Holy Guardian Angel, which according to Aleister Crowley is the higher-self of every person, who facilitates communication with the spiritual world.

**Aura:** The subtle energetic field that facilitates the flow of life energy in and out of the body. Psychics see the auric field radiating in rainbow-like color around the body. Sometimes the aura can be grey or black, as well.

**Bioplasmic Energy or Bioplasmic Field:** This is the dense, nearly physical energy field around a person which can be manipulated, condensed and directed. It is this field that provides energy for the physical manifestation of spirits.

**Ceremonial Magic:** A form of spirit communication that involves working with angelic beings. It is derived from Hermetic grimoires and Western esotericism and often includes elaborate rituals.

**Chakra Centers:** This is a network of major and minor energy centers. These are swirling vortices, which can be used to energize and heal the body.

**Demons:** Dark spirits who can be harmful or helpful to mankind. They are the fallen angels of Hebrew myth and possibly the Annunaki of the Sumerians. They are sometimes simply called "angels" as in the case of the Enochian angels contacted by John Dee and Edward Kelley. This term, also, refers to low level dark energies and thought forms, which are usually malevolent and appear as shadows.

**Ectoplasm:** An accumulation of bioplasmic energy produced by a physical medium, which enables spirits to enter this world in physical form for the duration of a séance.

**Elementals:** Entities and intelligent energies associated with the four basic elements, which are the foundation of life on the physical plane: Earth, Air, Fire and Water. Such beings are: Undines, Sylphs, Salamanders, Gnomes and fairies.

**Ghosts:** Spirits of the departed. They differ from angels, demons and elementals in that they were once living, although some ghosts are animal spirits.

**Life Force:** This is the subtle electricity that runs through the universe, animates all life, connects all things and makes spirit communication, magic and life itself possible. It is called by many names: Magnetic fluid, Odic Force, Ka (Qui or Chi), prana, orgone, astral light, dynamic ether, subtle energy, tachyon energy, etc.

**Magic:** An ancient, esoteric science that has a lot in common with modern quantum physics. It deals with a dynamic ether, frequencies, waves and resonance. The foundational theory is that there is a life force energy that runs throughout the universe and takes different forms.

**Magick:** This spelling of the word usually makes reference to ceremonial magic, especially Aleister Crowley's methods. As the language changed and mentalists like Houdini went on witch hunts for charlatans, Aleister Crowley devised this spelling to distinguish esoteric practices from those of stage performers, who a few hundred years earlier might have been called "jugglers."

**Medium:** A person who acts as an instrument of communication for spirits.

**Plane:** A bandwidth of frequencies that comprises a common reality, similar to a bandwidth on a radio dial.

**Psychic:** A person who is able to sense that which is beyond the common physical bandwidth of frequencies experienced by most people in the dense earthly plane.

**Spirits:** Any incorporeal entities.

# ABOUT THE AUTHOR

Angela Kaelin is the author of metaphysical books, such as, *How to Read the Tarot for Fun, Profit and Psychic Development for Beginners and Advanced Readers*, *The Traditional Witches' Book of Love Spells*, *Spells for Money and Wealth*, and *Magical Healing: How to Use Your Mind to Heal Yourself and Others*. She is, also, an alternative health writer and the author of *All Natural Dental Remedies: Herbs and Home Remedies to Heal Your Teeth & Naturally Restore Tooth Enamel*.

# MORE WINTER TEMPEST BOOKS

*All Natural Dental Remedies: Herbs and Home Remedies to Heal Your Teeth & Naturally Restore Tooth Enamel* by Angela Kaelin

*Black Magic for Dark Times: Spells of Revenge and Protection* by Angela Kaelin (Fiction)

*Blood and Black Roses: A Dark Bouquet of Vampires, Romance and Horror* by Sophia diGregorio (Fiction)

*The Forgotten: The Vampire Prince* by Sophia diGregorio (Fiction)

*Grimoire of Santa Muerte: Spells and Rituals of Most Holy Death, the Unofficial Saint of Mexico* by Sophia diGregoiro

*How to Develop Advanced Psychic Abilities: Obtain*

*Information about the Past, Present and Future Through Clairvoyance* by Sophia diGregorio

*How to Read the Tarot for Fun, Profit and Psychic Development* by Angela Kaelin

*How to Write Your Own Spells for Any Purpose and Make Them Work* by Sophia diGregorio

*Magical Healing: How to Use Your Mind to Heal Yourself and Others* by Angela Kaelin

*Natural Remedies for Reversing Gray Hair: Nutrition and Herbs for Anti-aging and Optimum Health* by Thomas W. Xander

*Practical Black Magic: How to Hex and Curse Your Enemies* by Sophia diGregorio

*Spells for Money and Wealth* by Angela Kaelin

*To Conjure the Perfect Man* by Sophia diGregorio (Fiction)

*The Traditional Witches' Book of Love Spells* by Angela Kaelin

*Traditional Witches' Formulary and Potion-making Guide: Recipes for Magical Oils, Powders and Other Potions* by Sophia diGregorio

**Disclaimer:** The author and publisher of this guide has used her best efforts in preparing this document. The author makes no representation or warranties with respect to the accuracy, applicability, fitness or completeness of the contents of this document. The author disclaims any warranties expressed or implied. The author of this book is not a medical or legal professional and is not qualified to give medical or legal advice. Nothing in this document should be construed as medical or legal advice. The material in this book is presented for informational purposes only. The procedures described in this book should not be used a substitute for treatment from state approved, licensed medical authorities.

Nothing in this book should be construed as incitement to dangerous or illegal acts and the reader is advised to be aware of and heed all pertinent laws in his or her city, state, country or other jurisdiction. Any medical or legal questions should be addressed to the proper medical or legal authorities. The author shall in no event be held liable for any losses or damages, including but not limited to special, incidental, consequential or other damages incurred by the use of this information. Always take proper precautions with candles, sharp objects, essential oils, herbs and use only as directed.

The statements in this book have not been evaluated by any other government entity. The statements contained herein represent the legally protected opinions of the author and are presented for informational purposes only. Anyone who uses any of the information in the book does so at their own risk with the understanding that the author cannot be held responsible for the consequences.

**FTC Disclaimer:** The author has no connection to

nor was paid by any brand or product described in this document with the exception of any other books mentioned which were written by the author or published by Winter Tempest Books.

Made in the USA
Lexington, KY
07 October 2013